STAND STILL IN THE LIGHT

poems by

Milton J. Bates

Finishing Line Press
Georgetown, Kentucky

STAND STILL
IN THE LIGHT

Copyright © 2019 by Milton J. Bates
ISBN 978-1-64662-026-5 First Edition
All rights reserved under International and Pan-American Copyright Conventions. No part of this book may be reproduced in any manner whatsoever without written permission from the publisher, except in the case of brief quotations embodied in critical articles and reviews.

Publisher: Leah Maines

Editor: Christen Kincaid

Cover Art: Elizabeth J. Bates

Author Photo: Elizabeth J. Bates

Cover Design: Elizabeth Maines McCleavy

Printed in the USA on acid-free paper.
Order online: www.finishinglinepress.com
             also available on amazon.com

                    Author inquiries and mail orders:
                          Finishing Line Press
                              P. O. Box 1626
                       Georgetown, Kentucky 40324
                                U. S. A.

Table of Contents

Forty-Six Degrees North

Naturalized 1
In Wildness 2
Tragedy at Presque Isle 3
Dendrolycopodium 5
Road Kill Retro-Loop 6
October Snow 7
Breakfast at the Huron Mountain Bakery 8
Tracking Snow 10
Transmigration 11
Since You Asked about Our Deck Lights 12
Translation 13
Lake Superior Levitations: Winter 14
Sublimation 16
Superior Ice-Out 17
Thaw 18
Skeleton Found in Ore Dock 6 19
Animal Faith 21
Intravenous 22
A Twilight Moonrise 23
After the Fall 24
Forty-Six Degrees North 25

Field Trips

Chinese Folk Song Performed on Oldest Playable Flute 29
Laundry Day in Burano 30
An Artist's Anatomy 31
The Discretion of Freud's Reading Chair 33
Defiance 34
The Votary 35
Wallace Stevens at the Cliffs of Moher 36
Apotheosis 37
Coyote Country 39
Windbound with Dostoevsky 40
Chosen 41

As They Were

Landing on the Moon 45
First Blood 46
As They Were 47
Sure-Footed 48
Football in Chu Lai 49
Vigil 50
Short-Timer 53
Listening Post 54
Man of God 55
Trick or Treat 56
Mantra 57
R&R 58
Payback 59
Re-Entry 60
Salt and Sweet 62
Kodak Moments 63

Passages

All the Sad Men 67
Dangling 68
Summer of '63 69
Selfie at Sixty-Five 70
Downsizing 71
Oral History 72
Bereft, He Chooses a Grave Marker 73
Détente 74
Barista 75
The Darkroom 77
Crossing the Waters 78
Paper or Plastic? 79
Introspection 80
Totaled 81
Supposing the House Is on Fire 82

for Puck

Forty-Six Degrees North

Naturalized

Approaching our feeder for the first time,
the gray squirrel was wary, ready
to retreat if challenged. Until then

the place belonged to birds and red squirrels.
What was a gray doing among our balsams,
pines, and spruces, far from the nut trees

it favored? We assumed it was just
passing through, a youngster perhaps, off
to see the world before it settled down.

Then it reappeared with another gray.
The pair made their nest, not in the hollow
of a hardwood or hammocked on an oak branch,

but high in the crown of a white pine.
They share the Jacob's ladder of its trunk
with nuthatches and brown creepers. The reds,

though still standoffish, observe the truce
declared each winter around the feeder.
Our neighbors are as surprised as we are,

hearing about the grays. *Any sign
there'll be a litter of little ones this spring?*
they ask when we meet them on the road.

That's the kind of people they are, happy
to indulge our minor discoveries.
More momentous was the one we made

many years ago, first passing through,
when we realized our question wasn't really
a question: *What if we chose to live here?*

In Wildness

> *In wildness is the preservation of the world.*
> —Thoreau

The wildness of a Lake Superior wave
drives deep water shoreward, building
until it stumbles on an upward lift
of sandstone. A frothy snarl precedes
                         the break and wash.

Through trunk and bough the fountain
of a hemlock's wildness surges
toward the light, hemmed in by other
hemlocks, browsed in winter by
                         rack-ribbed deer.

Without a howl to vent its wildness
the wolf would burst its lungs. That bellows
blast is throttled down by windpipe,
massaged by vocal cords, fine-tuned by
                         tongue and palate.

What do we know of wildness, we who call
it neighbor? We know the drive, the surge,
the bellows blast; and we know too well what
trips it up, what hems it in, what throttles its cry
                         in our throats.

Tragedy at Presque Isle

For Wendy Wickstrom, 1977 -1998

60 feet

First there were two of them, cranking
mountain bikes along the bluff.
Then one was plunging by herself
toward Lake Superior, pursuing
a separate fate. No Olympic
flourishes, just dead weight in free fall,
Newtonian, accelerating
at thirty-two feet per second
per second. Which falls faster, bike
or body? She would know the answer
when it no longer mattered.

40 feet

Layers of sandstone flickered past
like the strata of concrete block
seen through an elevator window,
but red with hematite, the color
of dried blood, older than she was
by thousands of years, yet still shifting
and tipping, still dropping crumbs
and people into an ancient sea
whose level had also fallen,
leaving a relic of its basin
high and dry, an almost-island.

20 feet

So many trails to choose from: why
that track outside the warning signs
and fence? Because her friend went first,
because at twenty she had life
to squander, because it was

forbidden. Any of these, or all,
or none. *Tragic but preventable*,
the newspaper editor would write,
echoing the police chief. But she
was forty feet beyond prevention.

10 feet

Beyond tragedy too, and all
things merely human. Gravity
gripped her in its talons like
a big-winged bird and took her
to a time before the personal,
before any creature could say
I am. Ceasing to resist, she felt
nothing, thought nothing, when the bird
released her in the shallows.

Yet grief is human. It was grief
that found her body, grief that nailed
a shingle with her name and earthly
span to a tree atop the bluff,
where hikers and mountain bikers
sometimes pause to parse it out.
They wonder who this Wendy was
and why the sign is there, so high
above the lake that if you toss
a stone you'll never hear the splash.

Dendrolycopodium

Nothing attracts less attention than complete success.
      —Bernd Heinrich

There's an understory to the understory
in our woods, a stand of trees so small
you may not notice them, or if you do,
mistake them for seedlings of the hemlocks
and spruces reaching for daylight high above.

Call them ground pines for their spiraling,
needled branches; or club moss for their raised
batons, and you'll be half right. But they're not
pines or mosses. Nor are they wolves, despite
a genus name that means "wolf-footed."

They've been prowling the earth on shaggy,
paw-like shoots since the Carboniferous.
A near relation, Lepidodendron,
invented wood and soared a hundred feet
above amphibians and steamy swamps.
When Lepi went extinct, leaving only
coal and fossils, our lycopods took note.

They flourish in the shade and wreckage
of more ambitious trees, the overreachers
that invest in sky-scraping structures
to capture sunlight, risking storm and drought,
insects and rot, the beaks, teeth, and saws
of creatures after heat and housing.

They are the Poor Richards of our woods.
Press your ear against the ground and listen
to the maxims pulsing through their rhizomes:
Keep a low profile. Live within your means.
Let others spread the news of your success.

Road Kill Retro-Loop

Except for a seething rice of maggots,
the twisted rag of fur and flesh
lies still beside the highway, *nature morte*.

Then the implausible happens:
ravens land and drop the eyes back in,
lustrous black and fat as plums.

The coat zips up and swells with meat.
Enamel brightens on the teeth.
The hooves glisten with wet lacquer.

A bloody ten-yard smear connects
the carcass to a car speeding in reverse,
its headlights diminishing to pinpricks.

The creature takes the impact in mid-stride.
Then with hind legs levering backwards
it retreats tail-first into the woods.

There it pauses, looking past the highway
at a moonlit trail leading to a cornfield.
The plum-eyed doe can see exactly

where it has to go. It levers forward
on its haunches, steps onto the pavement,
and takes the impact in mid-stride.

October Snow

We thought the blaze of red,
yellow, and orange that swept

our maple woods could burn
no brighter, until a shower

of early snow turned the color
up another notch. The leaves

caught and briefly held the cold
confection, serving it like sherbet

to the sultan sun. When the snow
slid from those fiery plates,

it left on each a slick as though
to mark the passing of a snail.

We marked that passing too,
that moment of millefiori

which had never been before
and never will be again.

Breakfast at the Huron Mountain Bakery

They face each other across the table
like opposing linemen, their heads
tucked into hunched shoulders,
their fists gripping coffee mugs.

It's always the same table,
a booth that commands a view
of parked cars. The patient grills
stand in formation, looking back.

At the front counter we share
a smile of recognition as we pay
for our coffee, redeye as usual,
and the usual toasted bagels.

Some things never change:
the coffee, the bagels,
the soft-eyed woman who
fetches them before we can order.

Also, of course, the Loud Guy
and his friend. *So whaddya think
of the new millage? Where will
it end?* Too loud, much too loud.

The room holds its breath
as though the answer matters.
The friend's mouth moves
inaudibly. What does he think?

Where will it end?
His half-hearing partner
nods, reading answers in
the pantomime of lip and brow.

Beyond the ranked grills,
well beyond, rises the knob

for which this place was named.
Forged in fire and ice,

it has been quiet a long time.
The Loud Guy, too, will be
quiet for a long time.
Some things do change.

This morning, though,
he is still in full voice.
Sliding into our booth, the usual,
we silently cheer him on.

Tracking Snow

Let there be a season when the earth,
prolific in spring, summer, and fall,
relaxes long enough to notice what
its offspring are up to—the foxes
that patrol the woods at night, imprinting
dotted lines in radii from their den;
the deer whose dainty trails turn into troughs
by February; the grouse that burrow
into drifts and then explode like land mines
when nearly stepped on; the dried grasses
that whip this way and that, stroking
Chinese characters onto the blank page.

Let there be a season when the earth's
outer skin is fluent as water, its waves,
ripples, and eddies forming and re-forming
as the wind veers around the compass;
when flake turns to liquid and liquid
to crystal in minutes. Let there be a season,
just one, when the earth attends to such
minutiae, when its surface is sensitive
as photo paper, a whiteness that tracks
its creatures' comings and goings.

Transmigration

To the jay it must have seemed as though
a thunderbolt had struck it from its perch.
It lay in the snow beneath the feeder, stunned,

after the other birds dispersed. So many eyes,
yet none had seen the dark comet coming
through the balsams. The chosen one resisted

briefly as the sharp-shin's talons probed its breast
and throat. Then it relaxed, its black eyes
focused on the distance like a martyr

or jihadist contemplating paradise.
It hardly felt the beak that rummaged
through its down and ripped its belly open.

Shifting its grip, the hawk hauled out
the smoking viscera, tugging as a robin
tugs at earthworms. It dipped repeatedly

for meat, for heat, for fluid in a frozen world.
Bit by bit one life became another.
What lifted off and flew away was neither

hawk nor jay but both, a mythic bird.
A plaque of feathers marks the place of rapture,
sky-blue with dabs of black and white.

Since You Asked about Our Deck Lights

We're not the kind of people who cling
to Christmas trees until Valentine's Day
or, God forbid, St. Patrick's. The tinsel,
the ornaments, the angel whose halo
grazes the ceiling: those we're ready to shed
before our balsam sheds its needles.
Yet we're loath to lose its nimbus of light.

Stripping the tree of bulbs one year,
we couldn't bring ourselves to pack away
the string outside our window, entwining
the deck rail like ivy. Each fall since then,
weeks before the solstice, we've wrapped the rail
with light. It's our defense against the dark
on moonless nights—not the city kind,
relieved by street lamps and neighborly
windows, but the black obliteration
that stalks our country homes in winter.
On waking, we flick a switch and watch
the thing jump back a good ten feet. We do
the same when it creeps back at twilight.

We snuff the bulbs earlier each morning
and light them later each evening
until one day in March they stay unlit.
That's when we dismantle our perimeter,
coiling the cord like concertina wire.
Christmas promises so much it can't
deliver. We do our little bit to help,
making in the darkness an outpost of light.

Translation

Four stanzas of firewood
stand in our backyard,
half-cords bracketed
by cribs of criss-crossed logs.

Between those end-stops
the rounds and splits speak
a common language, maple,
audible on windless days.

This is what they say:
Once we were a living body
basking in the solar fire,
our leaves articulate as tongues.

Now we are only bones,
moldering and all but mute.
Speak for us, set us aflame,
and we will keep you warm.

Lake Superior Levitations: Winter

i. Moonrise

Someone lights a lamp
in an igloo where
polar ice and sky
converge. The dome is
veined with gray and blue.

Through night's dark tunnel
the Trans-Siberian
Express approaches.
Its single Cyclops
eye reddens the rails.

A silver coin hangs
in space, suspended.
Heads or tails? There'll be
no winners tonight,
no losers either.

ii. Sunrise

A barn is burning
on the horizon.
Its flames extinguish
stars and warm the ice
from blue to salmon.

A mob ran riot
in the streets last night,
smashing windows. Shards
of glass divide and
multiply the light.

Shadows and rabbits
retreat to snow caves.

Smudging the whiteness,
A lone coyote
makes it whiter still.

Sublimation

> *We travel the Milky Way together,*
> *trees and men.*
> —John Muir

The orange, air-starved flame inside
my woodstove paints the window black.
When the stove gets hot enough to sear
the contour lines from fingertips,

that soot will turn to spirit, ghost
of maple, and fly up the chimney.
Two years split and stacked, the wood
is well seasoned, full of all it drank

from soil and air: carbon from the leaves
and seed wings of a bygone season,
carbon from the power plant upwind,
where black rocks burn to light my house.

The glass begins to clear. I picture
the big white pine that looms above
my chimney, leaning in as though
to warm its boughs, inhaling CO_2.

That pine has saved up several tons
of carbon. I'm good for thirty pounds
in flesh and bone. It's ours to keep, man
and tree, till fire turns us both to ghosts.

Superior Ice-Out

Living by the lake, we don't trust returning
birds to tell us winter's over. We watch
the ice and listen. For weeks we've heard
it whoop and detonate offshore, seen
the plates it's piled into windrows. More
docile now, it fractures quietly along
its fault lines. Water shows like ink between
snow-dusted geometric panels—squares,
rectangles, diamonds, trapezoids.

Then a wind disturbs the slabs, blurring
the neatly ruled lines. We look away,
distracted for a moment by less
momentous goings-on, then look back
to find the landscape rearranged. The sheets
are gone, replaced by what? Dragon scales?
Acres of honeycomb? Salt craters from
a dried-up sea? Freighter pilots call it
pancake ice, making of our flesh-numbing lake
a flesh-searing griddle. The cakes crunch
and jostle, fizz and tinkle, their edges
growing rounder as they socialize.

That's our cue to creep from winter houses,
to blink in the mid-March sun like hostages
released. We walk our dogs and check our
mailboxes, bumping into neighbors
who look familiar, remembered from
another time and place. Our voices sound
unnatural when we stop to talk, a bit
too loud, as though we're trying to be heard
above the slosh and sizzle of the ice.

Thaw

Hearing trickles turn into torrents,
we know the bluff behind our house
is letting go of winter, flushing it down
a dozen gullies into Lake Superior.

A neighbor's woods appears to be on life
support. Plastic tubing links his maples
to a clearing where a fire burns beneath
evaporator pans. Our lives, too, could use
support, a little sweetness after months
of bitter. Why not connect those drip lines
directly to our veins and save the firewood?

Last week my brother showed me the blisters
on his palms, all he had to show for
shoveling crushed stone onto fifty yards
of liquid clay. The frost is unimpressed
by his exertions. It keeps welling up,
turning his driveway into a truck trap.

You and I have the luxury of nowhere
in particular to go. *Thaw,* we say,
drawing out the vowel as the sun
draws vapor from the crusty remnants
of snow in our backyard. We linger
over coffee after supper, savoring
the afterglow. Your hands lie relaxed
and open on the table, as though
to gather in what's left of daylight.

Skeleton Found in Ore Dock 6

i. October 19, 1988

Halfway down chute 18 it hangs
like a cocoon waiting for spring
to trigger the transformation
plotted in the larval DNA.

But this is fall, and the raveled
chrysalis of parka, jeans,
and tennis shoes, derelict as
the dock itself, holds only bones.

Two summers have cooked the juices
off; two winters have freeze-dried
the skin and meat. Empty sockets
stare unbelieving upward

at the catwalk that gave his feet
the slip. Today two boys intrepid
as he was but more sure-footed
will find a missing person

before he's even missed. He'll be
a one-week wonder in the news,
delivered nameless and stillborn
from Number 6's rusty loins.

ii. April 1986

When he stepped from the hotel porch
onto Spring Street, he left it all
behind: the months in foster care,
the miles of pointless wandering

between Mount Clemens and Marquette.
Left or right? The rising sun drew

him toward the lake, for it was spring
despite the soiled rags of snow.

He could feel the randy buzz
of new beginning in his bones.
Today he would slough Tim Allain
off, lose that loser's wasted years,

all seventeen. Ahead, colossal
legs and hips rose from the water,
inviting him to mount and enter,
daring him to be reborn.

Animal Faith

If God is a merganser—and who's to say
He isn't?—our nesting pair may get a break
this year. Last spring they discovered
the big birch a storm decapitated long ago,
leaving the white column of its trunk to weather
like the last pillar of a Roman temple.

Rain and snow, freeze and thaw, mold and rot
scooped out a nest-sized hollow at the top.
The birds trimmed it out with feathers,
laid a clutch of eggs, and settled in to wait.

Their holidays were few and much the same,
a giddy glide from nest to lake, landing
with the kind of splash you have to pay for
at a water park. The trick was how to come
and go without disclosing an address.
Nature loves guile as much as patience.

They seemed to have the knack. An eagle
hunted daily from a dead snag at their doorstep,
unsuspecting. Then one day the snag was full
of crows, converging like gangsters on a bank.
That's how we knew the eggs had hatched,
that crows are smarter than eagles and mergansers.

Will the mob show up again this year,
shrugging their thuggish shoulders on the snag?
Our ducks take turns on the water slide.
They skim the lake for minnows and insects.
They are devious and patient, confiding
in a providence we find inscrutable.
We trust in our God too, our money says so,
but we have our reservations. Come hatching
time, we'll see which species got it right.

Intravenous

She swells with one red drop,
a distillation of my making.
Rivulets of DNA converge
from far-flung parts of Europe,

thinned slightly by the anti-
coagulant she injected
into my arm. For her it's merely
protein, propellant to spin

her offspring through the cycle
from egg to larva, larva
to pupa and finally adult.
Males swarm the evening sky,

tracing figure eights or tumbling
through space, joined briefly
to females. So many random
couplings, so many vectors

of life and disease. My mosquito
withdraws her straw and lifts
heavily off, an airborne tanker
with a raft of eggs to launch

on stagnant water. What mischief
will my blood breed? I neither can
nor want to know. Scratch an itch,
they say, you'll only raise a welt.

A Twilight Moonrise

In memory of John Dapra

The chairs are still there, John, but the magic
is gone. Gliding past them in my kayak,
I recall how you performed, one summer

evening, a moonrise over Lake Superior.
Through ferns and bunchberries you led the way
to a sandstone mezzanine already set

with wine and cheese. We waited—Puck and I,
you and Karen—for the theatre lights to dim.
You checked your watch once, twice, and then, maestro,

it seemed as though the spectral disk emerged
on the downbeat of your baton. *Voilà
la lune!* You acknowledged our applause

as your star attraction lifted red and ripe
above the horizon. That was ten years
ago. You'd think that someone who controls

the moon could handle anything, could even
dodge the pitch that got Lou Gehrig. Today
the chairs are yours no longer, nor the house.

The magic too is gone, except on summer
evenings when that other wizard rises
from the lake and conjures up your memory.

After the Fall

I still expect to see it every morning,
framed by my east-facing window: a hemlock
snag reduced to its essential form,
the charred skeleton of an ancient fish,
planted head down, tail up, beside the lake.

Long since dead and riddled with cavities,
the tree was more alive than most of those
still living. I marked seasons by the birds
that hunted from its spars: crows and ravens
in the summer, sharp-shins and merlins
fall and spring, eagles any time of year.

Like a sundial it told the hours of daylight,
showing first in silhouette, a crooked nerve
on the predawn retina. Then sunrise flamed
its tip, and light inched down and halfway
round the trunk. It crept back up at sunset.

One night that candle guttered out for good.
What's missing from my world? I wondered,
until an eagle winged by without pausing.
The colossus lay toppled on the shore,
its wood too punky-porous to burn.

Now my window frames an absence no one
seems to notice. *What an awesome view,*
guests say, looking out. And I agree,
remembering the flaw that made it perfect.

Forty-Six Degrees North

There is nothing to do, nowhere to get.
We need only "stand still in the light."
—Theodore Roszak, quoting George Fox

On those autumn days
when there is nothing to do
after the firewood is stacked
and the garden put to bed,
we do nothing

except bear witness
to the spectacle. The sumac
catches fire first, its red igniting
the maple's red and yellow,
the aspen's shaking gold.

On those winter days
when there is nowhere to get,
when the sun's low arc
barely clears the treetops
or the air is busy with snow,
we get nowhere,

content to watch the hemlocks
blur in the noonday dusk,
to wonder how our fire finds
another season's warmth and light
in slabs of beech and oak.

On those endless days
in spring and summer
when twilight lingers like
the final bugle-note of taps,
we keep vigil on a bench
beside the lake.

Our garden is planted,
the supper dishes put away.
There is nothing to do,
nowhere to get,

so we sit perfectly still,
observing how the birches
catch light from the water,
how their leaves become words,
how the words become poems.

Field Trips

Chinese Folk Song Performed on Oldest Playable Flute

It was all about air, how it passes
over mortal things. When the bone was
still fleshed and fledged, it made a slight
creaking sound as the great bird flew
over mountains. It lay mute and folded
as the bird stilt-walked the marshes
or clamored with the other red-crowns,
their slender bills pointing skyward
like reeds along the Yellow River.

The bone survived the bird. A man
of Jiahu drilled seven holes for air to come
and go as his lips and fingers pleased.
Even then the bone sang its own song,
an elegy for cranes and men, as though
it could hear the coming silence, foresee
the nine millennia of midnight.

At last a hand reached out of light
to lift the bone, clay-clotted, from its grave.
Soon it felt lips again, and fingers,
teasing air into tendrils of melody.
It half-learned and half-remembered
how Little Cabbage missed her mother,
especially in the spring, when the air
was sweet with peach and almond blossoms.

Laundry Day in Burano

Her bent figure casts a shadow
like a question mark on the stone façade,
asking what it will cost to fly this flag
of independence, pinned with effort

to a flower box beneath her window.
Neighbors grant it a kind of privacy,
but touring paparazzi from Venice
stalk the piazza with lenses as long

as Pinocchio's nose, caught in a lie.
When several circle closer, sensing
something true and photogenic,
she toils toward the door on her cane,

leaving to picturesque Burano the blue
and yellow blossoms that bounce lightly
above the flower box, the underthings
that hang sodden and colorless below.

An Artist's Anatomy

Florence, 1507

He opened his notebook and sketched
the old man's head upon a pillow,
dwelling on the eyes that after a century
could still watch unflinching for
the final marvel of their own eclipse.

The man sat up and spoke. Never had
he known infirmity, he said, only
this weakness at the end. Still sitting
upright, he passed without a tremor, leaving
to Leonardo the mystery of "so sweet
a death." The nurses of Santa Maria
Nuova had it figured out: thus do
the righteous die *in odore sanctitatis*.

Risking a pope's displeasure, he took up
a scalpel, cutting and drawing, filling
page after notebook page with diagrams
of arm and shoulder. The tendons tugged
at levers much as ropes controlled
the movements of his flying machine.

Was it merely another contraption,
or a temple of the Holy Ghost? That odor—
was it sanctity or rot? He traced the cause
of death to organs starved of blood. So sweet
the death, so vile the thickened arteries
and veins, the liver "like congealed bran."

Where in all this squalor was the soul?
Still lurking in a chamber of the brain?
More likely it had flown its cage. He'd give
the pious ones their resurrection,
but would they know it when they saw it,

saw the old man's essence in a woman's cryptic smile, a young man's graceful gesture?

The artist wiped his instruments and turned the notebook page. He felt the sinews in his arm extend and flex, precisely as he'd drawn them. He felt his blood surge toward the pen and change to ink. Onto the page it flowed, still sweet, still carrying something like a soul.

The Discretion of Freud's Reading Chair

> *S.F. had the habit of reading in a very peculiar and uncomfortable body position. He was leaning in this chair, in some sort of diagonal position, one of his legs slung over the arm of the chair, the book held high and his head unsupported. The rather bizarre form of the chair I designed is to be explained as an attempt to maintain this habitual posture and to make it more comfortable.*
> —Felix Augenfeld

It was his gift or curse always to seek
the underside, the id that lurks beneath
the ego and super-ego, the naked lust
that drives our noblest deeds. His couch,
draped disarmingly in a Persian rug,
encouraged confession. Reclining
in a parody of ease, patients gave up
their secrets freely in free association.

The censored speech of books he found less
scrutable. He would choose one from the shelf,
arrange his body like a contortionist
in the chair designed by Augenfeld,
and hold the volume overhead, as though
trying to peek under the skirt of lofty
sentiment or reasoned discourse. It was
his gift or curse, inflicting much dis-ease.

Few pages escaped the penetration
of those gimlet eyes, neatly encircled
by spectacles. Yet their secrets and his
are safe with the chair. That Henry Moore
homunculus has never relaxed or told tales.
It still presides over Freud's study
in London, knowing more than family
or friend about the doctor's underside.

Defiance

Paris, 2016

Never mind the braying of police sirens,
their incessant hee-haw, hee-haw; or
the bells of Notre Dame intoning hour
and half-hour as though nothing is amiss,
as though there are no soldiers patrolling
the great square in front of the cathedral
and the gated park behind. They move
silently among the tourists in squads
of four or five, weapons at the ready,
watchful, yet looking no one in the eye.

Listen instead to the ruckus that rises
from the quay across the Seine, where
a marching band, high school kids in yellow
and black, has taken a stand. People squeeze
between bookstalls, lean over parapets,
crowd the bridges for a better view.
Those closest to the band link arms and sway
from side to side in time with the music.
The brassy blare of trumpet, trombone,
and tuba drowns out the low rumble of
patrol boat outboards. *Go ahead,* the horns
shout into the brazen light of early fall,
sifting through the aspens. *Go ahead
and plant your bombs. We refuse to hide,
refuse to live as though already dead.*

The Votary

As the sun sets over the Loire Valley,
it blesses the royal chateau in Amboise
with its last light. Below that eminence
the streets are sunk in shadow, including
the Rue Victor Hugo, where a woman,
herself a kind of shadow in a well-worn
unfashionable coat, approaches a café
and chooses a table facing the chateau.
She nods when a waiter looks her way:
yes, the usual. The champagne arrives
in a slender flute, which she positions
like a votive candle on her table.

Was it here that she came each evening
with her husband, dearly departed?
Or does she come to celebrate another
day of freedom from the monster she'd lived
with all those years? Or has she noticed
how the royal chapel of Saint-Hubert,
looming high above, seems to glow with
an inner light just before the shadows
claim it? Leonardo lies beneath
the chapel pavement, immortal in death.
Only the sky is still alight, still quick
with swallows, when the woman stands
to leave, placing what may or may not be
an offering beside her empty glass.

Wallace Stevens at the Cliffs of Moher

> *It was like a gust of freedom, a return to the spacious,*
> *solitary world in which we used to exist.*
> —Letter from Stevens to Barbara Church

Sure enough, they looked just like the photo
on the postcard, *the cliffs of Moher rising
out of the mist* until they became his father.
That much and more he had gotten into his poem.
When the mist burned off, he could see what

the camera had missed: the churning cream
of surf six hundred feet below, the gulls
and gannets improvising loops, the puffins
standing at attention on the sandstone
galleries, and all those people crowding

to the cliff-top, dropping coins in telescopes,
ignoring signs that told them whom to call
if they felt an urge to jump. The big man
felt an urge to leave before his poem
shattered on the rocks. He took a detour

through the gift shop to check out T-shirts
in his grandson's size. That's where he found
a postcard like the one that lured him
to the cliffs. He paid for card and stamp,
then followed the clerk's pointing finger

to a postal box. For whom this souvenir
of misty solitude and spaciousness?
He addressed it to a son of stone in Hartford,
hoping it would purge from memory
much of what he had come so far to see.

Apotheosis

> *I can still see that woman. She was riding*
> *the crest of this huge wave into the harbor*
> *mouth. Then she disappeared.*
> —Witness to the 1954 Chicago seiche

La Crosse to Michigan City

Marching southeast across Wisconsin,
the storm front did not hesitate when
it reached Lake Michigan. Its heavy boots
got the seesaw rocking—down on one coast,
up on the other, the waves sloshing back
and forth in the glacial basin. A five-foot
swell slammed into the Indiana shore,
then rebounded westward toward Chicago.

Michigan City to Chicago

Fishermen in Michigan City scrambled
to higher ground when they saw the storm
approaching, ominous as Judgment Day.
Anglers across the lake saw only
tranquil sky and water, the cool prelude
to a hot Saturday in June, perfect
for catching perch. The surge cruised toward them
like the bow wave of Leviathan,
swimming just below the surface. Then all
was chaos as the ten-foot monster breached.

Montrose Harbor

Shaped like a fishhook, the Montrose pier
was baited with seven of the eight who drowned
that morning. Most were swallowed quickly,
most not seen again until divers brought up
their bodies. One woman, though, was swept
into myth on the back of something

larger than herself, larger than her city.
She was sister to Europa, straddling her
milk-white bull. She was Chicago, mounted
on a beast she could ride but never tame.

Coyote Country

For Taylor Mitchell, 1990-2009

If she loved anything more than music,
her mother said, it was nature. That's why
she wouldn't have wanted her killers killed
for doing what coyotes do.
                         I thought
of that young folk singer, hiking alone
on Cape Breton Island, as they charged
toward me, churning up the snow, their eyes
on fire with the setting sun. Just then
a rabbit erupted from a swale between us
and juked around my boots. One coyote
followed left, the other right, so close
I could have stroked their fur.
                         So they were real,
those phantoms whose frantic yipping I heard
late at night in counterpoint to sirens,
as though that wail of human pain drove them
to hysteria. My island was no Cape Breton,
just a scruffy patch of county land
lapped on all sides by city. Not wilderness,
by any means, but not quite urban either,
if animals like these could live there
undetected.
              They were pacing around
a pile of brush when I caught up with them,
probing with paw and muzzle, too intent
to notice me. I was luckier in my
coyotes than she was, the day her love
of nature went unrequited.
                         Selfishly,
perhaps, I save my love for those who love
me back. Yet I would hate to lose the little
that remains of wildness where I live.
I left them to their hunt, returning home
by streets that seemed no longer so familiar.

Windbound with Dostoevsky

June 2012

When Duluth flooded and zoo animals
drowned, the polar bear escaped. Before it
fell to a drug-tipped dart, it gave city folk
the frisson of a wilder place. The storm,
undarted, lumbered north and east across
the big lake, where it caught up with us.

We beached our kayaks and pitched our tent,
then rolled into fetal balls and played dead.
All night the thunder growled and lightning
clawed the sky. The worst of it was gone
by morning, hunting other prey. We woke
to the soft chatter of rain on nylon.

What better time for Dostoevsky?
All day his story of Muishkin, the gentle
prince misnamed The Idiot, unfolded
in our tent. When the rain stopped I took it
with me to the shore. Did stone and water
care that Nastasia lay dead in the ruins
of her wedding dress? That Rogojin
would do hard labor for her murder?
That the prince was once again an infant?

Superior still churned when I closed the book,
as though trying to scrub the human pain
from granite walls. Would they be clean by morning?
If so, the lake might have us back. We would rise
refreshed, illiterate as serfs, and paddle on.

Chosen

Do you get to choose your totem, or does
it choose you? In the Cascades that spring,
mine chose me as surely as my parents

chose my name. The sun had cleared the snow
from a campsite on Jakey Lake, but wouldn't
linger long. Shrugging off my backpack,

I jointed up a fishing rod and hustled
toward a pool of twilight encircled
by snow and jack pines. A fallen tree

served as dock, inclining toward deep water.
Again and again I cast, my line catching
light like a spider filament. That's all

it caught, or so I thought, until I felt
the bird alight, its Brancusi form familiar
on my boot: a red-breasted nuthatch.

With tentative beak it tapped first the rivet
on a lace hook. No grubs or insect eggs
detained it there, so up my leg it climbed,

solving with its toes the mystery
of blue denim bark. Perhaps it liked
my jacket better, the wool akin to moss

and lichens. *Where to next?* the climber
seemed to ask when perched at last atop
my shoulder. I could see my face reflected

in the miniscule black bead of its eye.
Then, answering its own question, it flew
off in search of more productive trees.

I turned back toward camp, my trout pool drowned
in darkness. Can you feel at once diminished
and exalted? No bigger than a bird's eye,

yet larger for that eye's election?
I had caught what I needed there, and wished
my totem equal luck in foraging.

As They Were

Landing on the Moon

Later he remembered how he had watched
a moon mission named for the sun, Apollo,
while on leave before he left for Vietnam.

The Eagle has landed, Neil Armstrong said
as the module nestled into moon-dust.
Then he descended a ladder and leapt

his ungainly leap for mankind. With his
shipmate Buzz he planted the flag
and scooped up soil samples. The men

looked like turtles in their boxy backpacks,
their helmets the size and shape of TV sets.
But they could hop like kangaroos.

That was in July. Now it was October,
months after his own eagle had landed
on a planet stranger than the moon.

Stepping from the plane, he had seen a flag
already planted beside the tarmac,
hanging limp as seaweed in the liquid heat.

Did he expect applause from mission control,
crackling through static, for walking trails
that sucked at his boots and soul? He did not.

Yet he envied those moon-men the lightness
of their landing, their giddy frolic in lunar
talc, their blessed reprieve from gravity.

First Blood

Bien Hoa Air Base

From where they stood it had a jaunty look,
rocking from side to side like a bus full
of restless children. They had ridden others
like it to school and summer camp, but this
was olive drab, not orange-yellow, and rigged
with window grates to fend off hand grenades.

The airport shuttle carried troops both ways,
some to war, others to a Freedom Bird
back home. The new arrivals wondered why
the home-bound bus would creep so slowly
toward their stop. And why was the driver
hunkered low behind the wheel, his face
a mask of terror? Before the folding door
could spill its secret, they heard pounding feet
and someone shouting *Make a hole! Stand back!*

The MPs went to work with their batons,
then dragged the brawlers from the bus, handcuffed
and sullen. Blood clotted in their hair and stained
their fatigues. These children hadn't learned
how to play or kill together, black and white.

The newbies climbed aboard and took their seats
in silence. War comes in many colors,
they were thinking, not just the green on green
whose uniform they wore, whose *how* they
understood, if not its *why*. Now they knew
they hadn't left that other war behind,
the one in which their skin enlisted them.

As They Were

As you were!

The sergeant's voice was stern, peremptory,
unlike the weary drone he'd opened with:

This is Instruction Block Three hmnnn,
Chu Lai Combat Training Center hmnnn,
"Securing Your Perimeter" hmnnn . . .

The first mortar shell shattered his monotone.
It seemed to come from somewhere deep inside
the earth, burrowing furiously upward
until it punched through the floor of the Quonset
hut where they sat in rows. Then the roof
thundered with the heavy hail of jungle stuff.

Hit the deck!

They hit it just in time to feel the second
blast along the full length of their bodies.
The floor bucked again, and the walls did
something they'd never seen before, the metal
folding neatly inward like a bellows pleat,
then folding out, as though the building,
too, sucked in its breath and then exhaled.

The roof rattled as before, and all was
quiet. Block Three would have to wait.
Perhaps tomorrow they would learn
how to secure a perimeter, how to hit
the deck with grace and dignity, how to be
as they were before the war turned real.

Sure-Footed

Carlos was a moralist, which is why
the question made him stop and think:
Are you sure-footed in rough terrain? Fact is,
no one in our platoon was surer, walking point.
He had the eyes, ears, and feet of a feral cat,
alert for trip wire fine as spider filament,
disturbed earth, a sniper's safety clicking off.

The rest of him belonged to Western Civ—
Boy Scouts, church on Sunday, the Disney
flick *Pinocchio*. That's what nearly tripped
him up, taking the army aptitude test.
Because he was trying, he told us one day
on patrol, not to show an aptitude
for infantry. *Pounding ground in Vietnam?
Hell no! Bad enough they drafted my ass.*

Still, the question made him look around
the room. All those shaved, anonymous
heads bent over test forms. What if some
computer, blind as fate, took him at his word?
Groped the Braille of graphite dots and sent
another guy instead? It was rough terrain,
but his pencil landed like a cat on *no*.

Carlos grinned, hating the work but loving
the irony. *So here I am*, he said,
same as if I'd told the truth. Then he shrugged.
Don't mean nothing. Desk job can kill you too.

Football in Chu Lai

You could count on it, the game would be
brutal when they showed up red-eyed from
lack of sleep, wearing the welts of a night

among mosquitoes in a piss-fouled bunker.
The longer the mortars fell, the more intense
the play. The wind peppered their faces

with dust as they piled fatigue jackets
for boundaries on a godforsaken slab
of clay. After the coin toss it was skins

against T-shirts, both sides in olive drab
from belt to jungle boots. No anthem or
referees, no spectators besides the guys

in the guard tower, weary of watching
concertina wire. They played two-hand touch,
not tackle, but ferocious, dirty,

elbows to ribs and knees to groins. How good
it felt to see the enemy and know
the score. They played to hurt. They played to win.

Vigil

Vespers: 1800 hours

The M-60 machine gun, the Prick-25
radio, the M-61 fragmentation
grenade: all were good at what they did,
but pledged allegiance to no flag. For that,
they needed human help. When a truck
delivered them to a guard tower
on the perimeter, it also left
a three-man team to show the hardware
what to do. They reviewed the password,
synchronized their watches, and drew straws.
Then they called in a situation report:
all secure.

Compline: 2100 hours

M-60, to name him for the gun he humped
from truck to tower deck, drew the first watch.
He had witnessed curtains of colored light
rippling in the Minnesota sky at night,
yet he was awestruck at these auroras.
Across the bay Cobra gunships poured
torrents of tracer into the Batangan
Peninsula. So deadly and so seductive,
almost too much for a good Lutheran.
He strove mightily against temptation,
trying hard not to love it, though his voice
betrayed no struggle when he checked in:
sit-rep all secure.

Matins: 2400 hours

Radio knew a thing or two about rain,
coming from Seattle, but the monsoon
was something else, blowing sideways
into the tower. Wrapped in his poncho

on the wet deck, a flak jacket for pillow,
he dreamed bad dreams about the sapper
demo at the Combat Training Center—
how that Chieu Hoi, a VC defector,
stripped down to shorts and glided through
the concertina wire as though it wasn't
there. Remember, the sergeant told them,
watchers are also watched. Radio shivered
awake and spoke into the handset:
sit-rep all secure.

Lauds: 0300 hours

Frags smelled the freshness of a new day
before he could see it on the horizon.
Coming of age when and where he did,
call it Sixties USA, he was acquainted
with fragmentation. Yet he believed
in brotherhood, that connection like commo
wire that linked their tower to the others.
He believed, too, in an ancient order
of watchmen: Chinese soldiers on the Great Wall,
Masai warriors leaning one-legged
on their spears, Basque shepherds in the Pyrenees,
hermits in desert hermitages. This was
the hour they longed for when they stood guard
against barbarians, hostile tribes, wolves,
or Satan. In how many ways, how many
languages, they had said or thought it:
sit-rep all secure.

Prime: 0600 hours

Waiting for the deuce and a half to pick
them up, the men watched the sun rising
from the sea, the smoke rising from breakfast
fires in the hamlet. Farmers filed along

a paddy dike like ants on a mossy log.
Fishermen sculled bowl-shaped boats offshore,
stopping to cast nets that caught the light
like spider webs wet with last night's rain.
The hardware would return to the tower
that evening, indifferent as ever to awe,
fear, and fellow feeling. Another team
would tend it, reporting hour after hour
like monks chanting the office, as if
the mere repetition, the chanting itself,
could make their situation all secure.

Short-Timer

Our medic, Doc, had just thirty days
to go in-country. *I'm so short,* he said,
I need a ladder to reach my bunk.
His was the bottom bunk, where he'd taken
to packing and unpacking his field kit
half the night. He still hacked it on patrol,
don't get me wrong, but there was something
strained, off-key, in how he laughed at his own
short-timer jokes. *Medic!* we'd call out,
just to see him jump. That was another joke:
I'm so short I can't jump over a rat turd.

At ten days he replaced his calendar,
the one with Xed-out dates, with that picture
of a girl you saw everywhere in Vietnam.
Her tits were numbered 3 and 2. Her snatch
was number 1. *By then I'll be so short,*
Doc said, laughing hysterically,
she'll never know I've come and gone.

The morning Doc inked in number 2,
he wouldn't leave the hooch. The LT stood
over his bunk, shouting at the shape
beneath the blanket, *You WILL fall out for
patrol, shit-for-brains.* We were forming up
outside, so we could hear the blanket's
comeback: *I respectfully decline, sir.
Medical profile, sir.* Then it giggled.
I'm so short I can't see over my boot-tops.

Listening Post

At twilight the four filed outside the wire
and claymores, weighed down with radio,
grenades, and dread. On reaching their post,
they arranged their bodies back to back
in the too-tight hole, then clicked the handset
twice to signal they were in position.

He remembered what his grandpa used to say
when he tried to sneak up on the old man,
smoking in a busted cane chair on the porch.

As darkness dissolved all boundaries
they became a single sightless monster,
eight-eared, sorting out the jungle racket:
branches rubbing branches, rummaging
in the leaf litter, the spooky chatter
of a bird or lizard, the soundtrack
of a movie alien as the landscape.

They'd hunted squirrels with .22's before
his grandpa's eyesight dimmed. The stillness
of the oak woods didn't fool them. Five minutes
into listening, they'd hear claws on bark.

They listened in shifts, one pair on, the other
off, drifting in and out of sleep. Shortly
after midnight the soundtrack switched off.
Elbow nudged elbow nudged elbow all around
as the silence grew loud with menace.

He remembered what his grandpa used to say,
sitting in that cane chair: I hear you coming.
You can't surprise me. I hear you coming.

Man of God

Minutes after a soldier left the Quonset
hut, the chaplain couldn't remember
the guy's name or why he'd come. A skag
or booze monkey on his back? A Dear John
letter? Compassionate leave for a funeral?
Qualms about collecting VC ears?
So mundane, and so unlike the ministry
he'd prepared for in the seminary,
where he imagined himself a Jeremiah
or Ezekiel, denouncing God's People
for straying from the path of righteousness.
A voice crying in the wilderness.

But whom to cry against when his country
anointed him to be, not a prophet,
but an officer and a gentleman?
Captain's bars outshone the tiny cross
on his lapel. It was his calling now
to unsimplify the simplest of the ten
commandments: *Thou shalt not kill.* So he
forgot their names and why they came to him,
blotted out their faces. He patched up
their troubled souls and sent them back to kill
or be killed. It was the war, he told himself
in doubtful hours, the war that made him do it.

Trick or Treat

It was like Halloween, mothers with kids
drifting from house to house for handouts,
except that the houses were hooches
and the neighborhood an army base.
We hardly recognized the mama-sans
who polished our boots, scrubbed our fatigues,
and swept red dust from the plywood floors
so we could track it in again. Most days
they went about their work or gossiped
in groups, anonymous and almost
invisible in soiled white tops and satiny
black pajama bottoms. One day each year
they dressed in their most colorful clothing
and led little harlequins from door to door.

Suppose the calendar had been filled
with days like that, when they were honored
guests, not hooch maids, sharing what mattered
most to them. Would the war have ended
differently? It was a kind of Halloween,
a day for dressing up and fussing over
children. Yet also ominous. Where were
the husbands and fathers? Planting rice
or netting fish, the women would have said,
if asked. But we knew better than to ask.
On Halloween, like every day in Vietnam,
we understood the need for masks.

Mantra

There it is, they said, and meant it,
when there was nothing else to say
about the village vaporized

by a misplaced bomb, the patrol
shredded by artillery support,
the short-timer wasted by a booby trap.

There it was when a letter from home
said there was no home to return to,
when a platoon went over the edge,

shooting chickens and children.
There it was whenever explanations
did not explain. You could question

the whereness of *there* or the whatness
of *it,* but not the pure ontology of *is.*
Is refused to answer questions.

Syllables so often in their mouths
grew smooth and egg-shaped like
the pebbles along the South China Sea.

They chose streaked or speckled ones,
rinsed off the sand, and put them
in their pockets for good luck.

R&R

What could be more thrilling than the steep
descent into Kai Tak Airport, encircled
by harbor and high mountains? They found
hotels, changed into civvies, and fanned out
to patrol the neon streets of Kowloon.

Which was more exotic, the monastery
on Lantau Island or the sampan village
in Aberdeen? They traveled by bus
to a checkpoint on the Chinese border,
rode the Star Ferry to and from Hong Kong,
marveled at the view from Victoria Peak.

Bars with silken girls in Wan Chai, restaurants
with fine linen, shops with cameras, tape decks,
and watches: weren't these the most enticing
attractions? It was war booty, all of it,
some to send home, some to savor themselves.

Was there anything more delicious
than soaking in a tub? More luxurious
than sleeping late between clean sheets?
Little by little, they let go of Vietnam.

What could be better than these, better
than rest and recuperation? The word
for what they'd felt eluded them until,
back in Danang, they no longer felt it—safe.

But they remembered how they'd walked
the streets with eyes uplifted, not scanning
the ground for trip wires and rigged artillery
rounds. They remembered how, for five
whole days, they'd forgotten to be afraid.

Payback

Sanders, the Sand Man, was the shooter
on our recon team, the guy we counted on
to take a Victor Charlie's cares away
with a single round. Put him to sleep.
He was methodical, businesslike. Punched in,
did his job, punched out. No regrets.

Which isn't to say he had no fantasies.
Here's one he let us in on. Back in
The World, he would stalk the members
of his draft board, one by one. He'd lay
the cross-hairs like a blessing on a face—
a man's, let's say, taking out the trash,
or a woman's, starting up her car.

Those months of practice, punching in
and punching out, would do the rest.
He'd inhale deeply, release a bit, then
hold steady, his fingertip so wedded
to the trigger that he couldn't tell before
from after. Except there'd be no after,
no bullet smashing bone. Why kill,
he reasoned, if the killing didn't matter,
only the singling-out for death?

We jumped all over him, demanding,
*Not even a note? What's the point, if
they'd never know?* Because he'd let us in,
because the fantasy was ours too.
I would know, the Sand Man said, nodding
as though possessed of esoteric wisdom.
I would know I'd chosen them this time.

Re-Entry

i.

The plane was a flat stone that skipped
the Pacific from Bien Hoa to Okinawa
to California, eight thousand miles
of timeless space. Inside, they kept
a stony silence, thinking back,
thinking forward, sleeping. A stewardess
patrolled the dark aisle, her fragrance
promiscuous with sweat and jungle rot.

From Travis then to Oakland for processing,
like beef or pork. A cafeteria, fluorescent,
served steak dinners round the clock,
the processed feeding on the processed.
Thank you, thank you for your service.
Please place tray on conveyor belt.

A gate delivered them to freedom,
blinking in the January sun, back in time.
So this was The World, the fabulous realm
of GI dream and desire. The freeway pulsed
with traffic and adrenaline. *Have a good
life, man,* they wished each other, thumbing
rides or hailing cabs. *No, have a great one.*

ii.

Back in Berkeley, he rented a room
that smelled of carpet shampoo and stale
cigarettes. There he sloughed his uniform
like an outgrown skin. Unsoldiered yet
unassimilated, he slunk through campus,
conscious of too-short hair and shaven face,
of PX clothes and army-issue shoes.

He re-enlisted in the university,
knocked on an office door, and lobbed
a question toward the slit-thin opening:
was there an empty seat in the English class?
You're two days late, a bearded face shot back,
inspecting him from top to toe. *The term's
already started. Where on earth were you?*

Like a stone he skipped toward Telegraph,
glancing off the once-familiar places, sailing
into space. He was thinking back, thinking forward,
wondering where he was, where on earth he was.

Salt and Sweet

Alaska, 1998

Be careful what you dig up. That was
the lesson he took from the ravaged scrap
of plastic he found half buried behind
his tent. He scoured it clean in Icy Bay,
its waters a blend of salt from coastal tides
and sweet from rivers of melted ice.
What emerged had been a canteen once,
before a bear chewed off its cap and raked
its flanks with teeth and claws. He knew what
he would find when he turned it bottom up
and read the imprint: US 1966.
Army issue, like the one he'd carried far
from here, in a previous life.
                                He lay awake
that night in the dusk of northern summer,
listening to a glacier's calving thunder.
Rising before the sun, he made a breakfast
fire and read the warning on the canteen's
front: *Do not apply canteen to open flame.*
How they used to laugh at that. He applied
it anyway, the canteen and all it still
contained, watched it flare up in the fire,
clench like a fist, and drip in acrid drops
onto the coals. It was a kind of
consummation.
                      He was loading his kayak
when a bear approached the camp upwind.
It rose onto its hind legs and sifted the air
with upraised muzzle. Scenting something
not quite right, too toxic to ingest, it dropped
to all fours and shambled off the other way.

Kodak Moments

The new shirt was one too many for
a closet already crammed with clothes
that no longer fit or were decades
out of fashion. It was time to purge.
Momentum took over and carried him
from the garment rack to the shelves above,
littered with the jetsam of his life.

He was making progress, the castoffs
piling up for a trip to the thrift shop,
old calendars and notebooks filling a waste
basket, when he found a box of photos
excluded from the family album.
He sat on his bed and lifted the lid,
inhaling the faint bouquet of mildew.

Then he spread them out, images captured
with a cheap camera and processed cheaply
at a post exchange. The colors had faded
or turned into other colors. But there
was no mistaking the place: the sandbagged
bunker, the hooch with corrugated roof
and screens tarp-draped against the monsoon rains.

Familiar, too, was the soldier striking
poses with an M-16, his sleeves rolled up
to regulation length, a bandolier
across his chest, the brim of his boonie hat
trained up in front like the ratty Stetson
worn by Gabby Hayes in the TV westerns.
Good old Gabby, always the sidekick, the clown.

He wondered who had snapped those photos,
whether he was still alive. Suppose they
got together for a beer. Suppose he brought
the pictures and fanned them on the bar
like a winning hand. They would laugh and shake

their heads at the kid in the boonie hat. Laugh again, more thoughtfully, and shake their heads.

Passages

All the Sad Men

My father was a stranger the year
our Midwestern city celebrated
its centennial. Inspired by vintage photos
of bearded men who stared unsmiling
into the lens as though it were a gun
barrel, the mayor and aldermen ordered
all adult males to grow facial hair
or risk the pillory and ducking tank
in a kangaroo court. No exceptions,
not even for men whose freshly shaven
faces belonged, like their starched white shirts
and ties, their business suits and wingtips,
to the Fifties corporate uniform.
What a trial it must have been to call
on customers in non-centennial cities,
repeating with every handshake the same
tired jokes about their deviant grooming.

At home around the supper table
we watched a five-o-clock shadow darken
into midnight. You've seen the sun when half
eclipsed? That was my father's face, except
the lighted half was grim around the eyes,
like the faces in those old photos. We felt
sorry for him, for all the sad men who
walked our streets that year in the penumbra
of a distant orb. What cause had we
to celebrate until the shadow lifted?
We wanted the eclipse to run its course
and give us back, unmasked, the face we knew.

Dangling

In that time before jeans were de rigueur,
my best friend's older brothers wore black chinos
with miniature buckles on the back,
three fingers south of the belt. For this
useless appendage teen culture of the late
Fifties had found a function. If a guy was
going steady with a girl, the buckle, too,
was hitched. If he wasn't, the ends dangled
loosely in invitation. Though my friend
and I still watched the Mouseketeers on TV,
we wanted to be teenagers when we
grew up, like his brothers and the kids
on American Bandstand. Our school, ever
vigilant for hoods and greasers, forbade
ducktail haircuts but not black pants with buckles.

I saw my chance while back-to-school shopping
for eighth grade. My mother hesitated
long enough over buckle-backed chinos
to give me hope, until she realized
what that metal could do to the wooden backs
of our dining room chairs. So I languished
another year in boyhood as my friend stepped
up to teenhood. Otherwise, little changed.
His buckle remained unfastened, mine
nonexistent. We were both still available,
though we had yet to figure out what for.

Summer of '63

It was a freakish accident in gym class,
the last before graduation, that changed
my summer plans. I could still indulge
in dates and drive-ins, sunning at the beach
and concerts. But I couldn't take the job
I was counting on to save for college.
The gas station owner shook his head.
Who could use a kid with a broken hand?

My father, for one. He hired my good hand
to stain the half-log siding on our cabin
in the north woods. Somehow I managed
with one arm, moving the ladder to stay
in the shade, handling brush and bucket
while swatting deer flies. A plastic bag shed
splatters of stain from the bandaged hand.

Several days into staining, I stopped
feeling sorry for myself long enough
to notice I wasn't alone. Quail took
dust baths in the driveway. A woodchuck
waddled to the meadow from its den beneath
our shed. Bats and nighthawks skimmed insects
from the sky at dusk. A whip-poor-will
rehearsed a single phrase on its slide whistle.

Maybe you have to be broken just
enough to mend in ways you didn't know
you needed to mend. Fresh from high school,
I was still too smart, still too intact, to know
what I needed. The stain was barely dry
on the siding when I packed my gear
and drove one-handed back to the city.

Selfie at Sixty-Five

Who was he now, he wondered, studying
the face in the restroom mirror. What was
he supposed to do? For so many years

he had known the answers. He was the guy
who woke to classical music, showered
and dressed, made breakfast and rode the bus

to an office with his name on the door.
It was the name his parents gave him,
trailing letters that testified to what

he had learned and could barter for the things
he needed—the toast and eggs, the bus fare,
the house he shared with wife and children.

They were still a part of who he was
as he unscrewed his nameplate from the door
and crossed the hall to the restroom.

The mirror had a plan. Tomorrow, it said,
you will rise to no manmade music.
You will breakfast on the brightening sky.

You will begin to learn what you have yet
to learn, things that will buy you nothing,
add no letters to your name. You will breathe

the ether of unbounded space. You will dread
the starkness of your poverty until
you come perhaps to love it. Now please smile.

Downsizing

After the moving van drove off,
crammed to the tailgate with furniture
and boxes, we camped for a week
in the house where we had raised
two children, sleeping on the floor
in goose down bags, boiling water
on the stovetop for instant coffee.

Sunshine flooded our campsite
each morning, no curtains or blinds
to hold it back. It was good light
in which to work at making
the empty rooms appear still
emptier, sponging off smudges,
patching nail holes, repainting walls
an eggshell white. We abided
by the camper's motto, Leave No
Trace, assuming those who came
after us would want a blank page
on which to chronicle their lives.

Daylight was ebbing from the rooms
that last afternoon as we erased
our way toward the back door.
An hour later, we might have
overlooked the faint pencil marks
on the door frame, one side per child,
recording the ascent that lifted
them up and over the threshold.

Sentiment inclined us to spare
those markings. But we'd been camping
for a week in a place we loved,
learning to let go and do without.
We left no trace on either side when
we followed our children out the door.

Oral History

It isn't the beach assault in Normandy
that he finds hard to talk about, though it was
bad enough. His landing craft found the German
mine, lifted with its blast, and came down
with a crippled ramp. The troops were trapped
inside, wide-eyed with fear as bullets
clamored on steel and burrowed into flesh.
When they climbed free he found himself alone
with bleeding bundles and a shattered man
who begged him for the mercy of a fatal bullet.

He speaks freely of a moonless night
off Italy, threading a maze of mines,
wondering which would kiss his ship goodbye.
Another night, waking restless and out of sorts,
he paced the LCI from stem to stern,
uncertain what dark demon drove him.
Twice he paused and leaned against the rail,
hearing a sea-siren call his name; twice
he wrenched himself away and back to life.

Yet sorrow, choking sorrow, grips him
by the throat when he recalls a deserted
railroad platform at the Soo. No one to see
him off? Not until Tunisia did a letter come,
the first from home. His sister's words
still have the power to wound. Like a torn
and shaken envelope, he lets them drop:
Dear Harry, Hope your ok. Can you
spare $50? Need it soon. Thanks, Me.

Bereft, He Chooses a Grave Marker

Stone
would not do, granite or marble polished
to give back a face he knew too well,
etched with grief. Fine-grained as glass
or steel, impervious, it would tell
his fingertips too much, too soon,
about the permanence of loss.

Wood
it would have to be, red oak from a tree
like those that framed her garden. It would
weather like their marriage. It would need
attention. He would massage it weekly
with fragrant oil, feeling in its grain
the familiar texture of her skin.

Earth
would claim him too, so he would have
another ready for himself. With no one
to anoint them, the slabs would check
and warp, turn gray and crumble
into dust. This he could foresee.
This was how it had to be.

Détente

Neither couple could remember
what word or deed had tipped the balance,
but now they detected it in every lift
of eyebrow, every compression

of the lips. Without ceasing to be friends,
they had become enemies—fast enemies,
so to speak, or bitter friends. It was like
a Christmas truce observed year-round.

When they met in No Man's Land for drinks
or dinner, the men shook hands to show
they held no weapons. The talk was cordial
as before, despite a wary aspect

in the eyes, a readiness to parry
any thrust. How *triste*, they sometimes thought,
recalling the unguarded laughter
of a simpler time. Still, there were

compensations. *Love is patient*, Paul says
in First Corinthians, *love is kind*.
But can you count on it to feed the cat
when you're away? Collect the mail?

Water the plants? What bound them now
was something less than love but more than fear,
a treaty none acknowledged, yet none
could live without, least of all the cat.

Barista

I go there mainly for the coffee,
always hot and strong, though the girl
who filled my cup was also worth
the trip—cheerful, chatty, cute,
home from college for the summer.
She must have overslept, I thought
one morning, still befogged before
caffeine, until I remembered
the month. Of course. September. Gone.

Her replacement seemed relieved
at the simplicity of my need,
a redeye with no soda fountain
infusions. She was new to the job,
but not to life. The gray hair clasped
behind her neck, the hands that drew
the coffee from an urn, belonged
to someone closer to my age.

It was the touch screen register
that derailed her. She grew flustered,
then panicky. *Take your time,*
I wanted to say. *I've got all day.*
Everything will be all right.
Instead I looked away, feigning
interest in a stack of *Times* on
the counter. The world is not all right,
the headlines said. Never has been.

When the touch screen finally
came around, money helped us past
the awkwardness—what I gave her,
what she gave back in change, what I
dropped in the tip jar. Business as
usual. She would get what she
needed from her job. I would get
my redeye the next morning.

We would pretend that coffee was all
she had ever done or wanted to do,
that everything really was all right.

The Darkroom

When he needed to see things clearly,
he retreated to a walled-off corner
of the basement, switched on a red light,

poured potions from brown bottles into trays.
Then he fed a filmstrip into the enlarger
and twisted the lens until his world snapped

into focus. It wasn't as he remembered
it, not yet, but the photo paper's
silver salts would make it right again,

turn black to white and white to black. He threw
an image onto the light-shy surface,
counted down, and eased it into a tray.

A picture bloomed in the seiche-like sloshing
of developer. He bathed it in fresh water,
locked it in with fixer, and rinsed it off.

Under white light the likeness seemed true
enough, but not as true as one he'd glimpsed
before the grays turned black. He'd heard

of images like that, shimmering above
the polar ice or desert sand. Shapes that weren't
quite there. Things seen once, seen truly,

never seen again. He hung the print
to dry and climbed the stairs to daylight,
climbed slowly toward that other darkness.

Crossing the Waters

In memory of Charles Ganzert

What a story you told me, Chuck, about
the summer you traveled to Tennessee
for the Down Home Pickin' Parlor Festival.
The Red Clay Ramblers, the Highwoods
String Band, Robin and Linda Williams:
the hottest acts in old-time music,
together during the hottest days of '76.

Your gang of cloggers from Virginia
walloped the wooden stage for an hour,
sweated through the applause, and then
retreated to a tiny creek out back.
Head to foot you lay in those cooling waters,
your shoes beside you on the bank. You were
every inch the stellar lineup promised
by the posters. An amusing sight, you
called it, a memory that stuck with you.

As you lay last week in your hotel room,
stretched out unconscious on the floor,
I like to think your bleeding brain replayed
that scene from forty years ago. You were
with them again, the Hoorah Cloggers,
humming the tune to *Step It Out, Nancy*
in that refreshing little Jordan of a creek.

Paper or Plastic?

I choose paper, not for all the right reasons,
but because we're out of trash bags.
The paper ones fit beneath our kitchen sink
and need no receptacle to give them shape.
Maybe that's what the grocery bagger
likes about them too—the way their fixed,
predictable form shapes the random objects
streaming toward him on the checkout belt.

I watch him lay a foundation of cans
and bottles as the cashier scans my
purchases. Then he adds the produce,
meat, and cheese in interlocking layers,
nestling convexity into concavity
and finally capping the edifice
with bakery, eggs and a bag of chips.

The architect is middle-aged, sober,
and shy, the kind you hear described as slow.
He almost looks me in the eye when
I thank him, not that he needs anyone's
thanks or approval. He knows how adept
he is, and quick. He has reasons for working
as he does, and knows they are the right ones.

Introspection

Paddle deeper into the fog,
leaving behind the spectral shapes
of dock and shoreline.

Stroke soundlessly, as though stalking
a shy animal. When you see
nothing on all sides,

when you find yourself suspended
between sky and water, you have
arrived at its lair.

See that cave carved into the mist?
Enter without fear, for you know
the animal's name

as well as your own. Those questions
you wanted to ask? Ask them now,
before the creature

can escape, before the wind sweeps
away its tracks, before the sun
sets its cave on fire.

Totaled

Stepping from the car unscathed, I looked first
at where the road dropped off to blasted rock,
then back at the cedar posts strung like fish
on steel cable. How many had my Subaru
uprooted? The tow truck driver counted
seventeen, said it was a local record.

My Subie joined the wrecks at his garage,
another crumpled ball around the basket.
When I came inside to call insurance,
he handed me his card. Above his name
and number was an upbeat motto:
We meet the nicest folks by accident.

Waiting for my agent to pick up, I thought
of those I had met—the woman who stopped
to see if I was hurt, the cop she called for help,
the tow truck driver. Nice folks, every one,
but the nicest were those I'll never meet,
the crew that rigged a safety net between
that highway and whatever lies beyond.

Supposing the House Is on Fire

It's a game we play. *Suppose the house is
on fire,* we say. *What would you try to save?*
Our children aren't for saving anymore.
They've grown up and moved to houses of their own.
No pets either, to complicate the choice.

You open with the jeans you'd grab because
you've never had a pair that fit as well.
I counter with my lucky fishing rod.
We're just warming up, passing the time
until one of us plays the winning card,
the same one every game. We would rescue
our photos first, low-crawling through smoky rooms,
dodging the falling embers and sparking wires
because we can't bear to lose the story
pictures tell, the proof we've walked this earth.

We tried a retrospective once, gorging
nightly on prints and slides, devouring
digital images. We remarked how young
we looked, how peculiar our clothes, how we
really must return to destination x or y.
The surfeit left us still unsatisfied.

What's missing from the record? we asked
ourselves, and had to answer, *almost everything.*
It's a game we play, the picture-taking too.
Who would ever guess that we sipped coffee
as the sun came up, spent most days working,
touched each other in the dark? Pictures
don't lie. But they keep secrets, including
this one: the house is always on fire.

Acknowledgments

This collection includes poems that first appeared in the following publications:

Always on Fire (Five Oaks Press chapbook): Lake Superior Levitations: Winter, Sublimation, Superior Ice-Out, Totaled
As They Were (YellowJacket Press chapbook): Landing on the Moon, Vigil, Man of God, Trick or Treat, R&R, Salt and Sweet, Kodak Moments
Bellevue Literary Review: Short-Timer
Blueline: After the Fall
Broad River Review: Defiance, Payback
Climate of Opinion: Sigmund Freud in Poetry (IPBooks anthology): The Discretion of Freud's Reading Chair
Cloudbank: Barista
Dunes Review: Bereft, He Chooses a Grave Marker; Supposing the House Is on Fire
Encore: Prize Poems 2014 and 2015 (NFSPS anthologies): Chinese Folk Song Performed on Oldest Playable Flute, Transmigration
Evening Street Review: Summer of '63
Great Lakes Review: Windbound with Dostoevsky
Health and Happiness UP Magazine: Tracking Snow
The MacGuffin: Introspection
Midwestern Gothic: Skeleton Found in Ore Dock 6, Tragedy at Presque Isle
O-Dark-Thirty: Football in Chu Lai
Peninsula Poets: Animal Faith, Breakfast at the Huron Mountain Bakery, Chosen, Crossing the Waters, Détente, Forty-Six Degrees North, Oral History, Selfie at Sixty-Five, Since You Asked about Our Deck Lights, A Twilight Moonrise
Proud to Be: Writing by American Warriors (Southeast Missouri State University Press), volumes 3, 4, 5, and 6: As They Were, Mantra, Re-Entry, First Blood, Listening Post
Putting the Wild into Words (Save the Wild UP anthology): In Wildness
Rattle: Coyote Country
Running with Water (V Press anthology): Translation
The Southern Review: The Darkroom
Stirring: Road Kill Retro-Loop
Third Wednesday: An Artist's Anatomy
The Timberline Review: Sure-Footed
Wallace Stevens Journal: Wallace Stevens at the Cliffs of Moher

Walloon Writers Review: Naturalized
Waters Deep: A Great Lakes Poetry Anthology: Dendrolycopodium, Thaw

Milton J. Bates earned a doctorate in English at the University of California, Berkeley, and taught for thirty-five years, first at Williams College and then at Marquette University. His scholarly books include *Wallace Stevens: A Mythology of Self* (University of California Press, 1985), editions of Stevens' notebooks and miscellaneous writings, and *The Wars We Took to Vietnam: Cultural Conflict and Storytelling* (University of California Press, 1996). Since retiring he has published *The Bark River Chronicles: Stories from a Wisconsin Watershed* (Wisconsin Historical Society Press, 2012) and two poetry chapbooks, *Always on Fire* (Five Oaks Press, 2016) and *As They Were* (YellowJacket Press), the runner-up for the 2018 Peter Meinke Prize. He was the recipient of a Guggenheim Fellowship in 1989 and Fulbright lectureships in China (2000) and Spain (2006). He lives with his wife in Michigan's Upper Peninsula, where they enjoy the region's year-round outdoor activities.

www.ingramcontent.com/pod-product-compliance
Lightning Source LLC
Chambersburg PA
CBHW070549090426
42735CB00013B/3124